Aberdeenshire Library and Information Service
www.aberdeenshire.gov.uk/libraries
Renewals Hotline 01224 661511

RILEY, Peter D.

Floating and
sinking

Ways into Science

Floating and Sinking

Written by Peter Riley

W
FRANKLIN WATTS
LONDON·SYDNEY

First published in 2001 by Franklin Watts
338 Euston Road, London NW1 3BH

Franklin Watts Australia
Level 17/207 Kent Street
Sydney, NSW 2000

Series editor: Rachel Cooke
Assistant editor: Adrian Cole
Series design: Jason Anscomb
Design: Michael Leaman Design Partnership
Photography: Ray Moller (unless
otherwise credited)

A CIP catalogue record for this book
is available from the British Library

ISBN 978 0 7496 7682 7

Dewey Classification 532

Printed in Malaysia

Picture credits:
Images Colour Library p. 7t; Oxford Scientific Films/Deni
Bowm p. 6t; Pictor International p. 12;
The Stock Market/Lester Lefkowitz p. 6b
Thanks to our models:
Jordan Conn, Nicola Freeman, Charley Gibbens,
Alex Jordan, Eddie Lengthorn and Rachael Moodley

Franklin Watts is a division of Hachette Children's Books.

Contents

Float

Some things
float and some
things sink.

Leaves float
in a stream.

A ship
floats in the
sea.

Or **sink**

A pebble sinks
in a pond.

Soap sinks
in a bowl.

Sorting materials

Lucy has a collection of objects.

Each is made from a different material.

a plastic fork

a cork

a sponge

a coin

a marble

a wood block

a metal teaspoon

She wants to see which material will float and which will sink if she puts them in water. Lucy fills in a table with her predictions.

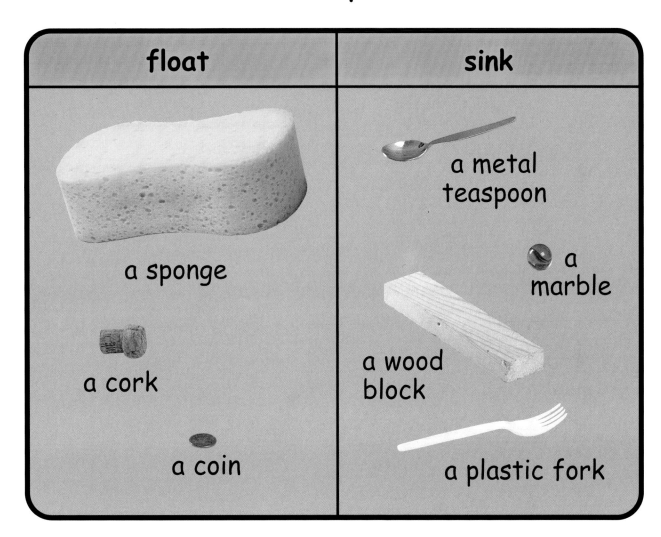

float	sink
a sponge	a metal teaspoon
a cork	a marble
a coin	a wood block
	a plastic fork

What do you think will happen? Write down your predictions too, then turn the page.

Which floats?

The cork, wood block and plastic fork floated.

The marble, coin and teaspoon sank.

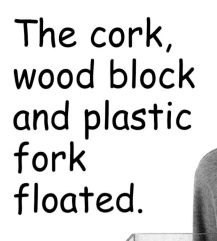

The sponge filled with water but floated just under the surface.

Were Lucy's or your predictions right?

Carl has a brick and a wood block about the same size. He tries floating them.

The wood is light in weight. It floats in water.

The brick is heavy. It sinks in water.

Water **pushes up**

Water pushes up on objects.

Water's push is strong enough to make lightweight materials like wood float. Even these large logs will float.

Feel the push of water yourself.

Screw the lid tightly on to an empty plastic bottle.

Push it under water.

Then take your hand away quickly.

What happens? Turn the page to find out.

Watch the water

The bottle rises quickly
through the water
and floats on
the surface.

The strong push of the water
makes the bottle move fast.

Pour some water into a clear bowl.

Put a mark at the top of the water-level.

Push an empty bottle into the water. The water-level goes up.

What do you think will happen when you take the bottle out?

Hollow or solid?

Some objects are hollow. They have air inside them.

An empty bottle is hollow. It is full of air.

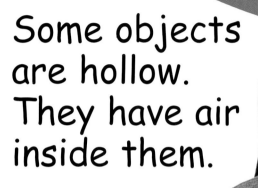

Hollow objects float because the air inside them makes them light in weight.

Some objects are solid.
They have no air
inside them.

If they are
made of a
heavy
material,
they sink.

a piece
of wood

a pebble

If they are made of a lightweight
material, they float.

Adam fills an empty bottle with sand. He puts it in the water.

Adam's bottle sinks. It is full of heavy sand and is not hollow any more.

Natasha puts a marble in an empty bottle.

She puts it in the water too.

What will happen to her bottle? Turn the page to find out.

Boats

Natasha's bottle floats. There is still lots of air in the bottle.

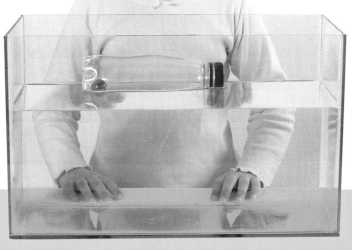

A boat is hollow. It has air between its sides.

When you put a small load into a boat, you push some of the air out.

The weight of the load makes the boat sink a little in the water.

If you put a very large load in a boat there is even less air.

The extra weight of the load is too strong for the water to push against and the boat sinks.

Take a ball of Plasticine.

Put it in water.

The ball is solid, not hollow, so it sinks.

Make the Plasticine
into a hollow dish.

Put the dish
in water.
It floats.

How small can you make the sides
and still keep the dish floating?

Boat loads

Adam has three 'boats'. Each one is made from a different material.

Each boat is about the same size.

A metal bowl

A plastic bowl

A polystyrene bowl

Adam tests them to see if they all float

He sees which boat can hold the greatest load.

He adds marbles to each boat until it sinks.

Which boat do you think will hold the least marbles?
Turn the page to find out.

Which  sinks?

The metal bowl sank first.

Adam made a chart of his results.

	polystyrene bowl	plastic bowl	metal bowl
first			✔
second		✔	
third	✔		

Try Adam's test. Are your results the same? Put them on a chart.

Try making boats of different shapes with the same amount of Plasticine and try Adam's experiment again.

Which shape holds the most marbles before it sinks?

Useful words

experiment - a fair test.

float - when something does not sink in water but stays on or near the surface.

hollow - when an object has empty space inside it, usually full of air.

load - the weight of the objects carried by a boat.

material - what objects are made from, for example: plastic, wood or metal.

prediction - a guess made before a test. The test will prove if the prediction was right or wrong.

sink - when something does not float on water but sinks to the bottom.

solid - when an object does not have any air inside it. A pebble is a solid object.

surface - the outside layer of something. Water's surface is where it meets the air.

water-level - the height water reaches in a container.

weight - the heaviness of something. A heavy thing pushes down more strongly than something that is light in weight.

Some answers

Here are some answers to the questions we have asked in this book. Don't worry if you had some different answers to ours; you may be right, too. Talk through your answers with other people and see if you can explain why they are right.

page 10 Lucy's predictions are right except for the coin (which sinks) and the wood block and plastic fork (both of which float). Your predictions may have been different from Lucy's so you may have got other ones wrong – or all of them right! Try the test for yourself using some different objects and use some new materials as well.

page 15 When you take the bottle out, the water-level will go down to where it was before the bottle went into the water.

page 23 The only way you can find out an answer to this is by testing Plasticine shapes for yourself. Try to make the Plasticine as thin as possible as this will help the boat float better – but be careful that there are no holes in its bottom.

page 27 Again the only way to answer this is to do the test yourself. Make sure the test is fair by using the same amount of Plasticine for each boat. Make a round boat, an oval boat and a square boat. Think about different shaped boats you find in real life. Predict which boat you think will hold the most before you start the experiment. Don't forget to make a record of your test results! Were your predictions right?

Index

About this book

Ways into Science is designed to encourage children to begin to think about their everyday world in a scientific way, examining cause and effect through close observation, recording their results and discussing what they have seen. Here are some pointers to gain the maximum use from **Floating and Sinking**.

• Working through this book will introduce the basic concepts of floating and sinking and also some of the language structures and vocabulary associated with it (for example, water-level and load, and comparatives such as hollow and solid). This will prepare the child for more formal work later in the school curriculum.

• On pages 9, 13, 19 and 25 children are invited to predict the results of a particular action. Ensure you discuss the reason for any answer they give in some depth before turning over the page. In most cases there is only one accurate answer, but don't worry if they get it wrong. Discuss the reasons for the answer they gave then create other scenarios and get the children to predict the results again.

• There are plenty of opportunities in this book to develop ideas related to force and movement. For example, the idea of weight as a pushing down force can be simply explored (pages 12 and 13) or the fact that objects the same size do not necessarily weigh the same (page 11).

• Even if you do not carry out the tests suggested in the book, you can use them to discuss and promote good practice in experiments. For example, if the containers on page 24 were different sizes, would this still be a fair test?

• When using the word solid, you may need to explore its other sense – solid compared to liquid or gas – which children may have met. If so, it is useful to discuss why we use the same word since the two senses are not unrelated.